ENGINEERING SUPER STRUCTURES

CANALS

PAIGE V. POLINSKY

Consulting Editor, Diane Craig, M.A./Reading Specialist

Sandcastle

An Imprint of Abdo Publishing
abdopublishing.com

abdopublishing.com

Published by Abdo Publishing, a division of ABDO, PO Box 398166, Minneapolis, Minnesota 55439. Copyright © 2018 by Abdo Consulting Group, Inc. International copyrights reserved in all countries. No part of this book may be reproduced in any form without written permission from the publisher. SandCastle™ is a trademark and logo of Abdo Publishing.

Printed in the United States of America, North Mankato, Minnesota

062017
092017

THIS BOOK CONTAINS
RECYCLED MATERIALS

Design: Kelly Doudna, Mighty Media, Inc.
Production: Mighty Media, Inc.
Editor: Rebecca Felix
Cover Photographs: Mighty Media, Inc.; Shutterstock
Interior Photographs: New York Public Library/Wikimedia Commons, Shutterstock, Wikimedia Commons

Publisher's Cataloging-in-Publication Data

Names: Polinsky, Paige V., author.
Title: Canals / by Paige V. Polinsky.
Description: Minneapolis, MN : Abdo Publishing, 2018. | Series: Engineering super structures.
Identifiers: LCCN 2016962862 | ISBN 9781532111020 (lib. bdg.) | ISBN 9781680788877 (ebook)
Subjects: LCSH: Canals--Juvenile literature. | Canals--Design and construction--Juvenile literature. | Civil engineering--Juvenile literature.
Classification: DDC 627--dc23
LC record available at http://lccn.loc.gov/2016962862

SandCastle™ Level: Transitional

SandCastle™ books are created by a team of professional educators, reading specialists, and content developers around five essential components—phonemic awareness, phonics, vocabulary, text comprehension, and fluency—to assist young readers as they develop reading skills and strategies and increase their general knowledge. All books are written, reviewed, and leveled for guided reading, early reading intervention, and Accelerated Reader™ programs for use in shared, guided, and independent reading and writing activities to support a balanced approach to literacy instruction. The SandCastle™ series has four levels that correspond to early literacy development. The levels are provided to help teachers and parents select appropriate books for young readers.

EMERGING • BEGINNING • TRANSITIONAL • FLUENT

CONTENTS

About Canals

Canals are human-made **channels**.

They are used all over the world.

The first canals were built about
6,000 years ago. They supplied
people with drinking water.

Farmers used
them to water
crops.

Canals were also used to **transport** goods.

Boats could carry many **items**.
And they could travel quickly.

Today, people still use canals to **transport** goods.

People also use canals to
supply water for drinking
and for crops.

The Panama Canal is famous.
It took ten years to build!
It opened in 1914.

The canal connects the
Atlantic and Pacific Oceans.

Engineers plan carefully to build a canal. They plan a fast **route**.

They dig the best
path for water
to take.

15

Some canals
are **shallow**.

But large boats need deep canals.

Canals must have plenty of water.

Rivers, lakes, and oceans
supply this water.

Workers clean canals. They clear **silt**. They clear trash. This is called dredging.

A clean canal can
last thousands
of years.

Think About It

Canals are used in many ways. What are canals used for where you live?

GLOSSARY

channel – a narrow stretch of water between two areas of land.

engineer - someone who is trained to design and build structures such as machines, cars, or roads.

item – a thing or object.

route – a road, path, or course that is followed to get from one place to another.

shallow – not deep.

silt – fine particles of soil that are carried by flowing water and then settle on the bottom of a river or lake.

transport - to move something from one place to another.